D0574253

It's Purim Time!

Latifa Berry Kropf
photographs by Tod Cohen

Thank you. . .

Once again to the staff, parents, and especially the children of Congregation Beth Israel preschool. You really know how to celebrate Purim with joy!

Dedicated to the CBI Purim Spielers of years gone by.

L.B.K.

Kar-Ben Publishing, Inc.
A division of Lerner Publishing Group
241 First Avenue North
Minneapolis, MN 55401 U.S.A.
1-800-4KARBEN

Website address: www.karben.com

Library of Congress Cataloging-in-Publication Data

Kropf, Latifa Berry.
It's Purim time! / by Latifa Berry Kropf ; photographs by Tod Cohen.
p. cm.
ISBN: 1–58013–153–0 (lib. bdg. : alk. paper)
1. Purim—Juvenile literature. I. Cohen, Tod. II. Title.
BM695.P8.K77 2004
296.4'36—dc22 2004005032

Manufactured in the United States of America
1 2 3 4 5 6 – JR – 10 09 08 07 06 05

It's time to celebrate Purim. We're building the king's palace in Shushan.

Let's pretend we're the people in the Purim story. Martin is making a crown so he can be King Ahashuerus.

Joseph is making a beard so he can be
Esther's Uncle Mordechai.

Julia and her friends are making a long, beautiful necklace for Queen Esther.

Jesse is cutting a mustache out of paper.
He wants to be Haman because everyone
makes noise when they hear his name.

Let’s look for costumes in the dress-up corner.

Mordechai found a black cape and Queen
Esther found a silky pink dress.

My teacher is helping me dress up as Haman.

Look! Two guards for Queen Esther's palace.

Look at Joseph. Now he's dressed up like a hamantasch.

It's time for a Purim parade!

Let’s make groggers.
First we decorate some cans.

Then we fill them with birdseed. When Purim is over, we can pour the seeds into our bird feeder.

When our teacher reads us the Purim story,
we shake our groggers every time
she says Haman's name.

There's so much noise we can't hear her.

Time for a snack. Ben is serving hamantaschen filled with strawberry jam.

Mmmm good!

On Purim we give *shalach manot,*
gifts of food, to family and friends.
Sarah was surprised to find Haman at her door.

Elly is giving shalach manot to Rabbi Dan.

*Chag Sameach**.
Have a Happy Purim!

*Happy Holiday

Recycled Groggers

What you need:

- Empty, clean, and dry soda cans
- Construction paper
- Stickers
- Glitter
- Ribbon
- Glue
- Duct tape
- Birdseed

What you do:

Wrap the soda cans with construction paper. Decorate with ribbon, glitter, and stickers. Fill cans up to halfway with birdseed. Cover the cans' open tops with duct tape.

These groggers can be used to teach about recycling and caring for the earth. We use leftover cans for our groggers, and when we're done, we feed seeds to the birds and recycle our cans once again!

About Purim

Purim, a holiday that comes in early spring, recalls the bravery of a young woman, Esther, and her cousin Mordechai. Without Esther's devotion to the Jewish people and her faith in God, the Jews of Persia would have been murdered. We find her story in the Book of Esther.

Children and adults celebrate this holiday by donning costumes, offering charity, and giving gifts (*mishloach manot**) to family and friends. An important part of Purim is to hear the reading of the megillah, a scroll containing the story, and to make noise with groggers, blotting out the name of the villain Haman. Hamantaschen, pastries shaped like Haman's three-cornered hat, are a favorite holiday treat. Parades, parties, and carnivals are also a part of the celebration . . . much fun for all.

*Mishloach manot is Hebrew for "sending portions." In Yiddish, the term is *shalach manos*, often Hebraicized to *shalach manot*.

About the Author

Latifa Berry Kropf has enjoyed teaching children since she started a summer nursery school in her parents' basement as a ten-year-old. She also loves to dance and sing, bake, and do art projects. She has a great husband and two wonderful, mostly grown-up children.

About the Photographer

Tod Cohen is a professional Day-in-the-Life photographer specializing in family and event photography. He loves working with children. Tod lives in Charlottesville, VA, with his two children, Gemma and Henry.